Explaining
What Happens
After Death

Roger Price

Sovereign World

Bible quotations, unless otherwise indicated,
are taken from the NIV The Holy Bible, New International Version.
© Copyright 1973, 1978, 1984 International Bible Society.
Published by Hodder & Stoughton.

NKJV New King James Bible.
© Copyright Thomas Nelson Publishers Inc.,
P.O. Box 141000, Nashville, TN 37214, USA.

AV Authorised Version of the Bible, Crown copyright.

ISBN: 1 85240 081 1

SOVEREIGN WORLD LIMITED
P.O. Box 777, Tonbridge, Kent TN11 9XT, England.

Contents

1

What Do People Believe About Death?

I hope you have noticed that the title of this book is not 'Explaining What Happens to a Christian After Death', but 'Explaining What Happens After Death'. The reason I have chosen this precise title is that I want to deal with what happens at death to the non-Christian, as well as to the Christian. Obviously, most non-Christians do not like to think about death very much and do not like being reminded about its reality. However, for them to ignore it is foolish, because death is the one and only certainty in their lives. We can all understand why they want to put it out of their minds, for we can probably all remember times when the reality of our forthcoming death really hit us. The sudden realisation that it will happen to us one day and that we will actually pass through it comes as a terrifying shock.

I still remember the time when, as a non-Christian, terrible fear gripped me as the reality and certainty of my death suddenly dawned upon me for the first time. I remember thinking, 'What a crazy thing this is! The moment a person is born, the only way he can leave life is by death and death is inevitable'. Nothing at all solves that problem. If you are alive and you want to get out of life, the only way you can go is via death. I thought, 'Well, there's absolutely no relief from this thing'. So I did what most people do. I consciously turned my mind away from it and tried to forget it as much as possible. I put it away as if it was not going to happen.

The problem was that death could not be kept away. The death of a close friend and the near misses of others only brought me face to face with death again. The reality of the shortness of life – that life comes to an end and that I really was going to die one day – refused to be ignored. Then I realised that the quicker it is faced the better.

"All come from dust, and to dust all return."

(Ecclesiastes 3:20)

For the sake of complete accuracy, I want to point out that it is absolutely certain that every non-Christian is going to die. It is also fairly certain that most Christians will die too. I say, 'fairly certain', because there will be one generation of Christians who will be alive on that glorious day when Christ Jesus comes for his Church; and those who are alive at his coming will not experience death, but will be raptured (snatched away or removed from the earth) and changed.

> *"Listen, I tell you a mystery: We will not all sleep, but we will all be changed – in a flash, in the twinkling of an eye, at the last trumpet."* (1 Corinthians 15:51-52)

> *"For the Lord himself will come down from heaven, with a loud command, with the voice of the archangel and with the trumpet call of God, and the dead in Christ will rise first. After that, we who are still alive and are left will be caught up with them in the clouds to meet the Lord in the air. And so we will be with the Lord for ever."* (1 Thessalonians 4:16, 17)

While many Christians believe that they will be in that number, beware lest you are believing it because you are afraid of facing death. Whether it is death or whether it is the rapture, Christians have **nothing** to fear. This is the good news of Jesus Christ: he conquered everything, including death, and has broken down the barrier that separated us from God. Death is one hundred percent certain, except for those who are going to be raptured.

I always remember an incident in the life of C.S. Lewis. He once had to talk to a group of soldiers who were on their way to join the British Expeditionary Force who were fighting on the continent of Europe. He stood in front of the nervous group and, discerning their fear, asked them why they were so frightened. The reason, of course, was because they thought that going to fight in the war increased their chances of dying. C.S. Lewis characteristically pointed out that going to war did not increase their chances of dying at all, for it was already one hundred percent certain that every one of them was going to die at some time or another. Some would die on the battlefield; those who survived and thought that they had escaped would find that death would still come sooner or later. All the war did was to bring the reality of death a little closer.

Quite recently, one of the last survivors of the Titanic disaster died – he avoided death in 1912, but eventually it came anyway. Other people have survived assassination attempts or cheated death for a time in some other way, but all discover that death comes in the end.

> *"There is a time for everything, and a season for every activity under heaven: a time to be born and a time to die."*
> (Ecclesiastes 3:1-2)

I often listen to a radio programme called 'Any Questions', which has a panel of celebrities who answer the various questions put to them. I remember one questioner asking a panel, which included the former leader of the British Labour Party, Michael Foot, the following question: 'Malcolm Muggeridge has said that he contemplates his own death every day. Do you think that is a good thing to do?' Michael Foot quipped, 'Yes, I think it's excellent to contemplate Malcolm Muggeridge's death every day!' When the question was answered seriously, he and two of the other three panellists explained that they felt it was not a good thing to do, but rather that we should fully occupy ourselves with life. The Bible, however, says that it is a good thing to contemplate daily how short life is.

> *"Teach us to number our days aright,*
> *that we may gain a heart of wisdom."* (Psalm 90:12)

Life is shorter than we think, and if we realised how rapidly it passes, many of us would change our lifestyle dramatically and be a lot more fervent in our Christian service.

But what happens when a person dies? If you ask ordinary people that question you will get a whole variety of answers. The majority would just shrug their shoulders and say, 'I don't know, and I don't want to talk about it anyway.'

Other people would express firm beliefs. Some, who are atheists, would express their belief in annihilation. By annihilation the atheist means that at the point of death, it is the end – everything just stops. Consciousness, feeling and existence cease from that time on. A person no longer exists. The philosopher Bertrand Russell believed this and many like him go very happily to their deaths thinking that there is nothing else to come. These people are in for the biggest shock in all the world.

Many people express a belief in reincarnation. This is in vogue these days and it is reckoned that thirty percent of the people of Britain now believe in reincarnation in one form or another. Many of these people have been influenced by the multitude of books on the market today detailing how people have had former existences. It is worth noting that the authors of these books have never had a humdrum former life – they never fed chickens or did the washing. They were always fighting in Cromwell's army or were King Philip II of Macedon or Julius Caesar!

Still other people would say, 'I believe there's life after death, but I'm not quite sure what form it takes.' This is rightly named 'agnosticism' (which means 'without knowledge').

The Bible definitely affirms that there **is** life after death and we must understand what it teaches. Christians are the only people who can actually speak about death with certainty. Christianity is unique because its founder, Jesus Christ, not only spoke about death and his victory over death, but also announced that he was going to die himself, and that after he had been dead three days he would rise from the dead. Thus, he would demonstrate that he had totally conquered death. True to his word, after three days he came back. So we know that the message he preached is certain. You do not get the same assurance anywhere else.

Mohammed died and we have not heard from him since – he has never been back to say, 'I told you I was right'. There is just an eerie silence. Buddha has not come back. None of the others have come back. They are still in their tombs.

But Jesus' tomb is empty. He embraced death and, having embraced it, then showed that he had mastery over it.

2

What Does the
Bible Say?

*"Man is destined to die once, and after that to face
judgement."* (Hebrews 9:27)

Do we see annihilation in this verse – that after death there is
just nothingness and a void? No! Do we see reincarnation? No!
We see instead two very clear and very important statements.

First of all, we see that men have one appointment with death
and one only. That stops the reincarnation theory dead in its
tracks. It does not say here, 'Man is destined to die five times'. It
simply states that man is destined or appointed to die **once**.

Second, we see that after death comes a frightening event: Man
has to face judgement. Darkness does not follow death.
Nothingness does not follow death. The event that follows death
is judgement. Judgement means that there **is** a life after death and
that after death we enter the courtroom of God to give an account
to him. These two things are stated as biblical certainties and
every person must reckon with them as such. We **are** going to die
and we **are** going to face God's judgement.

*"Then I saw a great white throne and him who was seated
on it. Earth and sky fled from his presence, and there was no
place for them. And I saw the dead, great and small,
standing before the throne, and books were opened. Another
book was opened, which is the book of life. The dead were
judged according to what they had done as recorded in the
books. The sea gave up the dead that were in it, and death
and Hades gave up the dead that were in them, and each
person was judged according to what he had done."*
(Revelation 20:11-13)

Is death 'the great equaliser' as many claim? It is not, because there is a difference after death between those who have believed in the Lord Jesus Christ and those who have not. This is clearly taught in two Bible passages.

First of all we must turn to the words of Jesus himself which clearly teach that there is life after death.

> *"Verily, verily, I say unto you* (that means 'of a certainty – this is absolute truth'), *the hour is coming, and now is, when the dead shall hear the voice of the Son of God: and they that hear shall live... Marvel not at this: for the hour is coming, in the which all that are in the graves shall hear his voice, And shall come forth; they that have done good, unto the resurrection of life; and they that have done evil, unto the resurrection of damnation."* (John 5:25, 28-29 AV)

'They shall hear' must mean that they will still have life and consciousness after death. If you do not have consciousness, you cannot hear! They **will hear** a voice.

In the Old Testament, we see the same thing expressed.

> *"And many of them that sleep in the dust of the earth shall awake, some to everlasting life, and some to shame and everlasting contempt."* (Daniel 12:2 AV)

When this verse says, *'**many** of them'*, it does not mean that there will be some who will not come forth. The Hebrew here just uses *'many of them'* to mean 'multitudes'. It means a vast number. We can put the word 'multitudes' in there (as many of the more modern Bible translations do); that is, *'And the multitudes that sleep in the dust of the earth shall awake'* – whether they are believers or unbelievers. There **is** a resurrection from the dead **for all**.

All the unbelievers who go to their deaths expecting annihilation are in for a great shock. The day will come when they too will rise from the dead. Philosophers, politicians, kings, actors, dictators, all the rich and famous, everyone will rise – that is the clear testimony of Scripture.

> *"They will have to give an account to Him who is ready to judge the living and the dead."*　　　(1 Peter 4:5)

We must also see that at this point of resurrection there is a clear divide between Christians and non-Christians – some shall awake to *"everlasting life"*, and some to *"shame and everlasting contempt"*. This is not 'pie in the sky when you die' either. This day is really coming. Every person who reads this book **will** be there. **Everyone** who has ever lived will be there. Those who have accepted Christ will rise to everlasting life, and those who have rejected him are going to find themselves under condemnation.

> *"Then they will go away to eternal punishment, but the righteous to eternal life."*　　　(Matthew 25:46)

The Bible clearly states that anyone who has trusted in Christ will not know condemnation. Their works will be judged, but the Christian as an individual will not be judged and condemned.

> *"There is now no condemnation for those who are in Christ Jesus."*　　　(Romans 8:1)

Christians do not trust in themselves or their good deeds to get themselves into heaven, but rather they trust in Christ Jesus. He has made the way, and Christians who have put their faith in him will go straight into heaven.

> *"Jesus answered, 'I am the way and the truth and the life. No-one comes to the Father except through me.'"* (John 14:6)

But those who have rejected Christ will find that things are very different. Their problem is clear. God is absolutely righteous and just and can have no dealings with sin. For a person to be accepted by God and dwell with Him in heaven, that person needs to have had his sin removed and to have the same righteousness as Christ. Even some Christians are confused about this and think that to have their sins forgiven is enough, but it is not. If you are a sinner and your sins are forgiven, that leaves you neutral. You were negative and now He has removed the negative. But the neutral cannot touch the positive, the absolute righteousness of God.

That is why Jesus not only forgave our sins, but he gave us a robe of righteousness as well.

> *"I delight greatly in the Lord; my soul rejoices in my God. For he has clothed me with garments of salvation and arrayed me in a robe of righteousness."* (Isaiah 61:10)

> *"God made him* (Jesus Christ) *who had no sin to be sin for us, so that in him we might become the righteousness of God."* (2 Corinthians 5:21)

Clothed in the righteousness of God Himself, we can approach Him. What a wonderful thing! And on that day we will find that we can look God straight in the face, because we have this garment of righteousness over us. Without His righteousness it would be impossible.

However, unbelievers will rise and will have no righteousness at all, only filthy rags.

> *"All of us have become like one who is unclean, and all our righteous acts are like filthy rags; we all shrivel up like a leaf, and like the wind our sins sweep us away."* (Isaiah 64:6)

God will recall everything that unbelievers have done in their lives in order to establish whether there are enough good deeds which, when all put together, add up to His own positive righteousness. Tragically, no one will ever be in that position. God will search and search, looking for righteousness equal to His own and He will never find it. So, the unbelievers will stand before God in a position of total condemnation because God cannot have them near Him. God cannot look upon that which is not absolutely righteous and, therefore, unbelievers will find themselves cast out.

> *"For the wages of sin is death, but the gift of God is eternal life in Christ Jesus our Lord."* (Romans 6:23)

The destination of those who do not attain God's righteousness by accepting Jesus Christ as their Lord and Saviour is what the Bible calls the second death.

> *"Then death and Hades were thrown into the lake of fire. The lake of fire is the second death. If anyone's name was not found written in the book of life, he was thrown into the lake of fire."*
> (Revelation 20:14-15)

The Bible clearly teaches that there is a divide between the believer and the unbeliever: outside of Christ Jesus the unbeliever has no way of overcoming the problem of sin and the resulting judgement of God.

3

The Rich Man
and Lazarus

Let us have a look at death itself. The people of the Old Testament saw death in a very specific way which can be seen clearly in the Old Testament and in the Gospels. Luke 16:19-31 is the story of the rich man and Lazarus and it gives us some important details about death. We must remember that the two main characters are two people who died before Jesus died on the cross, and are therefore Old Testament figures.

"There was a rich man who was dressed in purple and fine linen and lived in luxury every day. At his gate was laid a beggar named Lazarus (whose name means 'the hopeless one'), covered with sores and longing to eat what fell from the rich man's table. Even the dogs came and licked his sores. The time came when the beggar died and the angels carried him to Abraham's side. The rich man also died and was buried. In hell, where he was in torment, he looked up and saw Abraham far away, with Lazarus by his side. So he called to him, 'Father Abraham, have pity on me and send Lazarus to dip the tip of his finger in water and cool my tongue, because I am in agony in this fire.' But Abraham replied, 'Son, remember that in your lifetime you received your good things, while Lazarus received bad things, but now he is comforted here and you are in agony. And besides all this, between us and you a great chasm has been fixed, so that those who want to go from here to you cannot, nor can anyone cross over from there to us.' He answered, 'Then I beg you, father, send Lazarus to my father's house, for I have five brothers. Let him warn them, so that they will not also come to this place of torment.' Abraham replied, 'They have

Moses and the Prophets: let them listen to them.' 'No, father Abraham,' he said, 'but if someone from the dead goes to them, they will repent.' He said to him, 'If they do not listen to Moses and the Prophets, they will not be convinced even if someone rises from the dead.'" (Luke 16:19-31)

Let us note a few points from this parable of Jesus.

1. The rich man is depicted as not being a believer and, conversely, Lazarus is depicted as a believer who lived in abject poverty.

2. Both of these men have died and both are seen as conscious after death! This is very important. The Bible speaks of death in terms of sleep, but that normally refers to the physical body. Your physical body is said to go to sleep, but your soul is still conscious and awake and experiencing things after death. We will see what our souls are going to experience later on, but it is vital to see that after death we are still alert. The rich man and Lazarus were asleep as far as their physical bodies were concerned, but awake in their souls. In fact, this passage actually recounts a conversation which took place after the two men had died. They were conscious and able to feel, to reason, to see, hear and communicate. We all will be like this after death.

3. In verses 22 and 23 the parable speaks of 'hell'. Now it is vital that we understand this word, 'hell'. The word 'hell' is probably the most misunderstood word in the Bible. Most people think of hell as the place where unbelievers go, and they think of it as a fiery place which is awful. The truth is that the word 'hell', the Greek word 'Hades' and the Hebrew word 'Sheol', all simply mean the 'unseen state', i.e. the realm into which all who die pass. A place where they are still conscious, but in which those who are still alive cannot see them any more. In fact, in one of the creeds it actually declares that 'Jesus descended into hell'. Some people think that this means he went down into the place where the unbelievers were. However, it does not mean that. It simply means he went to the place where all the dead go. We can show 'hell' as a large circle:

Where the dead go

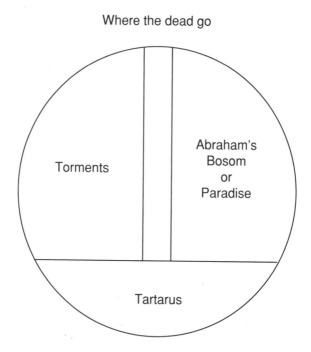

Verse 22 tells us where the Old Testament believers went. In the Authorised Version of the Bible it says, *"It came to pass, that the beggar died, and was carried by the angels into Abraham's bosom."* Here is the compartment in the unseen state which is called 'Abraham's bosom' and which is also known as 'Paradise'. 'Paradise' was a Persian word meaning 'the garden of the king'. It denoted a beautiful place, because the king of Persia had the most beautiful garden in the whole kingdom. That is the description of the part of the unseen state which was provided by God for believers in Old Testament times. Abraham's bosom simply meant 'resting in the arms of Abraham'. And so the moment the believing beggar died he was taken to Paradise and, figuratively, Abraham wrapped his arms around him. Notice, by the way, that Abraham is also alive in this place.

There is another compartment, however, into which the rich man went. In verse 23, the Authorised Version of the Bible says, *"In hell* (the unseen state) *he lift up his eyes, being in torments"*. *"Torments"* is the title of the second compartment of hell which was reserved for unbelievers. Undoubtedly, part of their torment was that the unbelievers could see what luxury and happiness existed over in Paradise. But *'Abraham's bosom'* and *"Torments"* were separated. In verse 23, the rich man sees *"Abraham **far away**, with Lazarus by his side"*. Also in verse 26 it further explains, *"between us and you a great chasm has been fixed, so that those who want to go from here to you cannot, nor can anyone cross over from there to us."*

For completeness, I will just deal briefly with the third compartment of the 'unseen state'. This third compartment is not dealt with in this passage, but I would give it the name 'Tartarus'. 'Tartarus' is only used once in the Greek New Testament, that is in 2 Peter 2:4. Here we have the little word 'hell' used again, but it is not the same Greek word for 'hell' as is used in other parts of the Bible. It is the word 'tartaroo' which we transliterate 'Tartarus'. This is the place where condemned and bound fallen angels go to await judgement. Specifically, Peter is talking about those demons who tried to upset God's plan back in the days of Noah.

> *"For if God did not spare angels when they sinned, but sent them to hell* (Tartarus)*, putting them into gloomy dungeons to be held for judgement; if he did not spare the ancient world when he brought the flood on its ungodly people, but protected Noah, a preacher of righteousness, and seven others...."*
> (2 Peter 2:4-5)

Here we learn very clearly that when the angels sinned and were judged in Noah's day, they were sent to this place called Tartarus.

4. It must be remembered that the gulf or chasm between Paradise and Torments means that no one can move over from one to the other. If you hear any person saying that after death you get a second chance, this passage clearly shows they are wrong. Wherever you go after death is the place in which you will stay until the Great Judgement (Revelation 20:11-15). How clear it is:

"'And besides all this, between us and you a great chasm has been fixed, so that those who want to go from here to you cannot, nor can anyone cross over from there to us.' He answered, 'Then I beg you, father, send Lazarus to my father's house, for I have five brothers. Let him warn them, so that they will not also come to this place of torment.'"

(Luke 16:26-28)

We can note from this passage that an unbeliever in Torments is still quite capable of honourable thoughts towards other people. Human good is still coming out of him. But the reply to this noble sentiment is definite:

"Abraham replied, 'They have Moses and the Prophets; let them listen to them.' 'No, father Abraham,' he said, 'but if someone from the dead goes to them, they will repent.' He said to him, 'If they do not listen to Moses and the Prophets, they will not be convinced even if someone rises from the dead.'"

(Luke 16:29-31)

What Abraham is saying, is that by reading Moses and the Prophets they could have come to a knowledge of the truth and a saving knowledge of the Messiah, Jesus, who was coming. When Jesus came there were many true believers in the land, people who had believed already, having read Moses and the Prophets. Anna and Simeon (found in Luke 2) were among them. It may be that some of the disciples were among them too, and that Jesus simply went and chose them and called them to follow him.

There is also irony in this passage. The rich man really believed that if someone had appeared to him from the dead **he** would have repented and so would his relatives. But Abraham told him the bad news that this would not be the case. Jesus **did** rise from the dead. He came back and yet people continued to reject him and remained unbelievers. It is not a lack of evidence, it is an evil heart of unbelief which causes people to remain in their unbelieving state. Today some would say that if we saw more miracles, more unbelievers would be saved. That is not true either. Jesus had a miracle ministry for three and a half years and ended his life rejected and despised.

18

4

The Death of Jesus

Luke 23 describes the death of Jesus and shows us the truth about death. Jesus did not cling on to life. Many people who are afraid of dying think they have to cling on to life. So long as they are alive, they are all right. But Jesus wasn't like this. Jesus could have hung on the cross for ten days. He didn't. The moment his work was done he said in effect, 'That's enough, it is finished!', and departed after only six hours on the cross. There was no fear at all in him, because he knew that there was nothing fearful about death. He went into death with full knowledge of the facts. We must not let the devil deceive us about death, because he is more frightened of it than we are.

> *"Since the children have flesh and blood, he too shared in their humanity so that by his death he might destroy him who holds the power of death – that is, the devil – and free those who all their lives were held in slavery by their fear of death."* (Hebrews 2:14-15)

In Christ we can have the same freedom that he demonstrated. He had no fear of death, either on the cross or in the Garden of Gethsemane. Jesus was not concerned about death while he prayed in Gethsemane, but rather was concerned about the torment that was coming his way – the suffering which he was going to experience on the cross. He was certainly not frightened about death. Death was the moment of triumph as far as he was concerned. It was with total ease that Jesus said in Luke 23:46, *"Father, into your hands I commit my spirit."* He knew exactly what he was doing.

Luke 23, verses 32 and 33 describes three crosses. Jesus was on one and two criminals were on the others. One man was innocent, the other two were very guilty. Verse 39 of the same chapter speaks of one of the criminals hurling insults at Jesus and mocking him saying, *"Aren't you the Christ? Save yourself and us!"* It is a very common experience for non-Christians who are about to die to start railing and shouting at God.

For example, I heard the testimony of a man who escaped from a burning aircraft. The aircraft had crashed and God delivered him alive. He said that one of the things that shocked him most was the way people were cursing God in the moment of their death. We would think that people would call on God to deliver them. The truth is that it is often the exact opposite which really occurs.

This thief was typical of many when he said, *"Aren't you the Christ? Save yourself and us!"* However, the other thief had a very different attitude.

> *"But the other criminal rebuked him. 'Don't you fear God,' he said, 'since you are under the same sentence? We are punished justly, for we are getting what our deeds deserve. But this man has done nothing wrong.' Then he said, 'Jesus, remember me when you come into your kingdom.'"*
>
> (Luke 23:40-42)

This was the point of his salvation. In the following verse, Jesus answered him with these wonderful words, *"I tell you the truth, today you will be with me in paradise."* This thief was a man who had spent his life sinning and defying God. He was guilty. But when he turned to Jesus in his last dying moments, Jesus said in effect, 'Today, you will be where I am going to go.' He was, from that instant, on his way to Paradise, which is the place where all the Old Testament believers were taken.

Notice that there is no question of purgatory. Jesus did not say, 'Well I'm glad you've turned to me. I might see you in a couple of years. You're going to be burnt up a bit and the dross is going to be removed, and then you'll just get through.' You do not find that. Rather, Jesus says, *"Today you will be with me in paradise."* The Son of God himself, who had lived a perfect life, said this to one who had lived an awful life. It is clear that the thief's deeds had been terrible. He even said of himself that he was justly hanging on his cross. Yet Jesus said that they would both be in the same place after death. Nobody could have any better news than this. Every one of us is guilty, but Jesus is able to save to the uttermost all those who turn to him. This is the marvellous good news of the gospel of Jesus Christ.

All men are actually made of three parts. We have a spirit, a soul and a body (1 Thessalonians 5:23). In his death, Jesus shows us what happens to these.

The following verse tells us what happened to his **spirit**.

> *"Jesus called out with a loud voice, 'Father, into your hands I commit my spirit.' When he had said this, he breathed his last."* (Luke 23:46)

The spirit, which is the part of us which gives us life, is the property of God and it goes straight back to Him. James tells us that *"the body without the spirit is dead"* (James 2:26). When a person dies, the spirit automatically goes back to the Father.

Jesus' **body**, as we well know, went to the grave. Joseph of Arimathea buried it and fulfilled the prophecy that Jesus was *"with the rich in his death"* (Isaiah 53:9).

His **soul** went to Paradise – the compartment of the unseen state where believers are sent. Some people believe that when Jesus went down into 'hell', he did more work. What they are saying is that when Jesus died on the cross, his work was not finished, because he had more work to accomplish in hell. However, this is not true. If this was the case Jesus would not have said, *"It is finished"* (John 19:30). He went down into the unseen state, but he went in victory having done all that he was intended by God to do.

> *"For Christ died for sins once for all, the righteous for the unrighteous, to bring you to God. He was put to death in the body but made alive by the Spirit, through whom also he went and preached to the spirits in prison."*
>
> (1 Peter 3:18-19)

21

Some Christians take this passage to mean that Jesus went and preached to the unbelievers, many of whom were then converted! We need to read the rest of this passage in order to get at the truth. The following verse goes on to define the spirits Jesus preached to as:

> *"the spirits in prison who disobeyed long ago when God waited patiently in the days of Noah while the ark was being built. In it only a few people, eight in all, were saved through water."* (1 Peter 3:19-20)

The mention of Noah shows us that the word 'spirits' doesn't mean unbelievers, but the literal spirits or demons which are locked up in Tartarus. Also, only eight people are spoken of as being saved. Salvation is something which is decided during a person's life, not in hell. Notice that the passage does not mention that these 'spirits' were saved.

It is vital to note the word 'preach' here too. Two Greek words are commonly translated as 'preach'. One is *'evangelizo'*, the other is *'kerusso'*. The first means 'to preach the gospel', the second means 'to proclaim the victory'. The word used in 1 Peter 3:19 is *'kerusso'*. Jesus didn't go and preach the gospel to these imprisoned spirits, he went to proclaim the victory. He went out of Paradise down to Tartarus, and when he got there he proclaimed to the demons the victory that he had won.

These demons had tried to cause Jesus to fail in his mission by polluting humanity so much that Jesus could not be truly human. It would not have been possible, had they succeeded, for Jesus to take on a human nature, because it would have been too defiled. However, the demons had failed and that was the good news Jesus preached to them. They had not had any news of the battle for quite a while, but the news was delivered by Jesus. He was not going to let another demon tell them. He was coming to do it himself. The sort of thing that Jesus would have proclaimed would be, 'I have won the battle. You are totally defeated and the only thing that remains for you now is total judgement. Noah will rise and he will condemn you.' Having done this, he went back to Paradise.

Why did he go to Paradise? He had a job to do there too. It was simply to tell the believers to prepare to move out. There was no more work to be done. He simply had to tell them what was going to happen next. So he appeared to them all and we can imagine his message, 'You've only got three days more here. We're moving premises.' When Jesus rose from the dead, every single Old Testament believer was taken up into heaven with him. More than that, even Paradise itself was taken up into heaven with him.

> *"But unto every one of us is given grace according to the measure of the gift of Christ. Wherefore he saith, When he ascended up on high, he led captivity captive, and gave gifts unto men."*   (Ephesians 4:7-8 AV)

The Authorised Version of the Bible puts it well when it says *"he led captivity captive"*. What does this phrase mean? This was used in the Roman Empire. An army was sent out to defeat, say, Gaul or Britannia, and after the battle the Romans would take a certain number of local people back with them as 'prisoners of war'. To show how great the victory was they had to show some living examples of the people they had been fighting against. They used to collect some of the worst looking specimens and bring as many home with them as they could. They would then appoint a day when they would have a celebration of the battle and of the victory that had been won. On this day all the soldiers would parade through the town and everyone would shower them with rose petals and such like. There would be tremendous cheering and, in the middle of the procession, the prisoners of war would be shown off, all chained together. As these prisoners passed, the citizens would realise just how great the victory was, and the cheering would get louder for the soldiers who came after them.

That is what is referred to in Ephesians 4:8 as taking *"captivity captive"*. So when Jesus returned to heaven, he paraded all of the 'prisoners of war' – believers that he had won from the earth. However, he wasn't showing off chained prisoners through the streets of heaven, but people who were free, totally free. He would have been saying to the angels, 'Aren't they beautiful?

Aren't they lovely?' This is what happened on the day of the resurrection. Paradise was totally emptied and transferred into heaven.

5

The Believer's Inheritance

What does this mean now for us who are believers? It means that we do not go down, we go up! We go up to heaven when we die. The unbeliever still goes down to Torments. The rich man we looked at earlier is still there. But Lazarus and Abraham are now up in heaven. Paradise has been moved into heaven. This is clearly taught in the following passage.

> *"I must go on boasting. Although there is nothing to be gained, I will go on to visions and revelations from the Lord. I know a man in Christ who fourteen years ago was caught up to the third heaven. Whether it was in the body or out of the body I do not know – God knows. And I know that this man – whether in the body or apart from the body I do not know, but God knows – was caught up to Paradise. He heard inexpressible things, things that man is not permitted to tell."* (2 Corinthians 12:1-4)

Here Paul speaks in a most mysterious way that is not found in any of his other books. He speaks as a man who has experienced such tremendous things that he dare not speak about them – and he hardly dares identify himself as that man. What he had seen in heaven was too wonderful for words. His experience was **so** awesome that he dared not describe it. All of us who are in Christ are going to have exactly this same experience when we die. I imagine that believers who die must think, 'Oh, if only I could go back and tell everyone.' The longing to do so must be tremendous. However, the truth is that those of us who are still here have to rely on the Holy Spirit to show us how wonderful heaven is.

When did this happen to Paul? It probably occurred when Paul was in Lystra on his first missionary journey.

> *"Then some Jews came from Antioch and Iconium and won the crowd over. They stoned Paul and dragged him outside the city, thinking he was dead."* (Acts 14:19)

It may well be that Paul actually died at that time. Certainly, those who had stoned him thought that this was the last they were ever going to see of him. If Paul did die at this time, it may also have been the time when he was taken up into heaven.

You will notice in 2 Corinthians chapter 12 that Paul does not even mention the stoning. It became as nothing compared with what he had seen. This is rather like what we read of Stephen in Acts chapter 7 verse 56, who, when he was martyred, could only say, *"I see heaven open and the Son of Man standing at the right hand of God."* Stephen forgot the stones which were raining down on him.

However, Paul's story continues,

> *"But after the disciples had gathered round him, he got up and went back into the city."* (Acts 14:20)

It appears that Paul rose from the dead. This was a miraculous event. The people of this time knew how to stone a man. They would not have left him half dead. Even the fact that Paul immediately got up and went back into the city is amazing. During the stoning his body must have suffered many broken bones and been badly damaged, but Paul got up and, the next day, was able to continue his missionary journey. An amazing miracle indeed!

Let us look at the passage in 2 Corinthians chapter 12 in more detail.

> *"I know a man in Christ who fourteen years ago was caught up to the third heaven. Whether it was in the body or out of the body I do not know – God knows."*
>
> (2 Corinthians 12:2)

Paul was too overcome by what was happening to him to know whether he was experiencing it in his body or out of it.

What then is the third heaven that Paul mentions? I believe that the first heaven is the atmosphere, the second heaven is the universe, and the third heaven is the Throne Room of God.

> *"And I know that this man – whether in the body or apart from the body I do not know, but God knows – was caught up to Paradise."* (2 Corinthians 12:3-4)

Paradise is now up above for us who are believers, because Paradise has been transferred to heaven. Unbelievers still go down, but believers go up. Therefore, look up, because that is where our hope is centred. We will be taken up at the point of our death, and we, like Paul, will hear *"inexpressible things, things that man is not permitted to tell."* (2 Corinthians 12:4).

> *"For as in Adam all die, so in Christ all will be made alive."* (1 Corinthians 15:22)

As far as believers are concerned, their spirits go to the Father, their bodies go to the grave and their souls go to the heavenly Paradise. That is why we are perfectly right to say, 'When a Christian dies he goes to heaven.' Our body may be asleep, but we are still conscious. We are conscious of Jesus. We will be wrapped about with the presence of Jesus and so we will experience eternal bliss.

> *"Brothers, we do not want you to be ignorant about those who fall asleep, or to grieve like the rest of men, who have no hope. We believe that Jesus died and rose again and so we believe that God will bring with Jesus those who have fallen asleep in him. According to the Lord's own word, we tell you that we who are still alive, who are left till the coming of the Lord, will certainly not precede those who have fallen asleep. For the Lord himself will come down from heaven, with a loud command, with the voice of the archangel and with the trumpet call of God, and the dead in*

Christ will rise first. After that, we who are still alive and are left will be caught up with them in the clouds to meet the Lord in the air. And so we will be with the Lord forever. Therefore encourage each other with these words."

(1 Thessalonians 4:13-18)

6

Better By Far!

As we grow older, we face accumulating evidence of our mortality. Through bereavement, and the increasing inability of our own bodies to do all that we ask of them, the inevitability of decay and death becomes more real to us. In the light of this, the writer of Ecclesiastes offers the following wisdom,

> *"Remember your Creator in the days of your youth,*
> *before the days of trouble come*
> *and the years approach when you will say,*
> *'I find no pleasure in them' –*
> *before the sun and the light and the moon and the*
> *stars grow dark, and the clouds return after the rain;*
> *when the keepers of the house tremble,*
> *and the strong men stoop, ..."*   (Ecclesiastes 12:1-3)

His conclusion contains an even more sobering truth,

> *"Here is the conclusion of the matter:*
> *Fear God and keep his commandments,*
> *for this is the whole duty of man.*
> *For God will bring every deed into judgement,*
> *including every hidden thing,*
> *whether it is good or evil."*   (Ecclesiastes 12:13-14)

What a fearful end awaits all unbelievers. Whether they believe that they will pass peacefully into oblivion or that somehow 'it will be all right', or whether the awful reality creeps up on them, the horror of that final moment of realisation is beyond comprehension.

A friend of our family told the story of her husband's death. She recounted that when her husband was on his death bed he suddenly cried out with a look of fear on his face, 'Oh, no!', and fell back dead against the pillow. That man seems to have suddenly realised the truth expressed in the following verse,

> *"Man is destined to die once, and after that to face judgement."*　　　　　　　　　　　　　　　(Hebrews 9:27)

I believe that this is the most fearful thing in the world.

The good news is that Jesus has come and offered us eternal life in place of death and separation from God.

> *"For God so loved the world that he gave his one and only Son, that whoever believes in him shall not perish but have eternal life."*　　　　　　　　　　　　　　　(John 3:16)

Jesus said,

> *"I am the resurrection and the life. He who believes in me will live, even though he dies; and whoever lives and believes in me will never die."*　　　　　　　(John 11:25)

The life which God offers us is the most precious and, yet at the same time, the most freely and universally available gift we can receive. The tragedy is that so many people reject it.

> *"Whoever believes in him is not condemned, but whoever does not believe stands condemned already because he has not believed in the name of God's one and only Son. This is the verdict: Light has come into the world, but men loved darkness instead of light, because their deeds were evil."*
> 　　　　　　　　　　　　　　　(John 3:18-19)

Compare the following two verses,

> *"'Do I take pleasure in the death of the wicked?' declares the Sovereign Lord. 'Rather, am I not pleased when they turn*

from their ways and live?'" (Ezekiel 18:23)

"Precious in the sight of the Lord is the death of his saints."
(Psalm 116:15)

Why does the Lord delight in the death of his saints? Because they come immediately face to face with Him. Having been absent from Him, they are then present with Him forever. The day of our death is a wonderful and exciting day as far as God is concerned, but I believe He weeps over all the unbelievers who die.

God expressed his love for us by sending Jesus to bear the judgement that was due to us because of our sin. He endured separation from God on the cross that we might enter the relationship with God that was intended for us from the beginning of creation. Not only can we know salvation from hell and freedom from the fear of death, but it has become possible for us to know God personally and to become part of His family.

In the book of Philippians, Paul expresses the assurance which comes from apprehending this truth,

"For to me, to live is Christ and to die is gain."
(Philippians 1:21)

We see no fear of dying in this statement. Paul knew exactly what was going to happen to him. In effect, he way saying, "When I die, I'm a rich man. The best thing that can happen to me is death, for that's the time when I really gain."

When Paul wrote these words he was in prison. He could not decide whether he would prefer to be executed or to be released from prison. I can imagine him walking up and down saying, 'Shall I die or shall I live? If the choice were mine, I wouldn't know which way to choose!'. What a decision! He wanted to go and live with Jesus, which was a far more wonderful prospect than anything else, but he knew that God might have further work for him still to accomplish.

"If I am to go on living in the body, this will mean fruitful labour for me. Yet what shall I choose? I do not know! I am

torn between the two: I desire to depart and be with Christ, which is better by far; but it is more necessary for you that I remain in the body." (Philippians 1:22-24)

The Bible says that we, as Christians, need have no fear of the day when God calls us home. It is the most wonderful thing that can happen to anyone who has trusted in the Lord Jesus. It is a thrilling thing to be with Christ. In fact, as Paul says, it is *'better by far'*.

Jesus has conquered death, he has conquered sin, and he has conquered hell. Therefore, the moment that we die, we will come into eternal bliss. In this state we will wait until the resurrection day to receive the resurrection body prepared for us. This resurrection body will be our home for ever and ever.

This is the hope of every Christian. If you doubt this truth or have no revelation of it, then the devil is robbing you and is lying to you. We have to resist his lies and refuse to be duped (James 4:7; 1 Peter 5:8-9).

King David was expressing the same hope when, in Psalm 23, he wrote,

"Even though I walk through the valley of the shadow of death, I will fear no evil, for you are with me; your rod and your staff, they comfort me." (Psalm 23:4)

When we are with the Lord, the 'shadow of death' is all we experience. It is rather like entering a valley where the shadow of the mountain falls on you. There is a world of difference between the mountain falling on you and the **shadow** of the mountain falling on you! When the shadow of the mountain falls on you, you are not crushed and you are not damaged in the slightest way. This is the implication of this verse in Psalm 23. For a shadow to fall on you, you have to be separated from the cause and there has to be a bright light shining. So we walk through the valley of the shadow of death. The fact is that it is the shadow of death only. This means that we are separated from death itself and it will never touch us.

The moment we are about to die, I like to think that Jesus

himself will appear before us as he comes to collect us. We saw earlier that this happened to Stephen in Acts chapter 7. He received a vision of Jesus as he was being stoned to death, and such was the impact of it that he was able to disregard the effect of the stones. I like to think that we too will see such a vision of Jesus that we will not notice death overtaking our physical bodies. We will be too enamoured with Jesus.

The Lord Jesus Christ has made it possible for us to walk through life now absolutely free from the fear of death.

> *"Since the children have flesh and blood, he too shared in their humanity so that by his death he might destroy him who holds the power of death – that is, the devil – and free those who all their lives were held in slavery by their fear of death."* (Hebrews 2:14-15)

We can now live our lives in hope of the coming resurrection.

> *"For the trumpet will sound, the dead will be raised imperishable, and we will be changed. For the perishable must clothe itself with the imperishable, and the mortal with immortality. When the perishable has been clothed with the imperishable, and the mortal with immortality, then the saying that is written will come true: 'Death has been swallowed up in victory'."* (1 Corinthians 15:52-54)

I pray that the Lord will release every person reading these words from any fear of death. Take these truths away; chew them over; digest them, and they will be like honey to you. You will find that they release you from any fear.

Jesus is Lord: he has conquered death and hell. Praise God! He rose from the dead and appeared again to demonstrate his victory. Knowing this truth we can be delivered from any fear of death, so that we might be free to live for him.

7

Living as
Eternal People

When Jesus walked on the earth, there were few people who failed to recognise that he was radically different from other men. We read that they were *"amazed at his understanding"* (Luke 2:47), that they *"marvelled"* at his miracles (Mark 5:20 NKJ) and that they were *"astonished"* at his doctrine and authority (Matthew 7:28-29 NKJ).

The disciples, who were closest to Jesus, were also perplexed by him, as the following account illustrates,

> *"Then he got into the boat and his disciples followed him. Without warning, a furious storm came up on the lake, so that the waves swept over the boat. But Jesus was sleeping. The disciples went and woke him, saying, 'Lord, save us! We're going to drown!' He replied, 'You of little faith, why are you so afraid?' Then he got up and rebuked the winds and the waves, and it was completely calm. The men were amazed and asked, 'What kind of man is this? Even the winds and waves obey him!'"* (Matthew 8:23-27)

The disciples' question *"What kind of man is this?"* was later to be answered by John, after he had seen the risen Christ:

> *"And the Word was made flesh, and dwelt among us, (and we beheld His glory, the glory as of the only begotten of the Father,) full of grace and truth."* (John 1:14 AV)

There had never before been such a man. Jesus, being both God and man, had brought God's eternal life into a fallen world.

"The life appeared; we have seen it and testify to it, and we proclaim to you the eternal life, which was with the Father and has appeared to us." (1 John 1:2)

But God's purpose was that the Son of Man would be *"lifted up"* on the cross *"that everyone who believes may have eternal life in Him"* (John 3:15). Thus, Jesus would become *"the firstborn among many brethren"* (Romans 8:29 AV).

Henceforth, those who put their trust in Jesus Christ would receive eternal life and know fellowship with the living God.

"Now this is eternal life: that they may know you, the only true God, and Jesus Christ, whom you have sent." (John 17:3)

As Christians, we can look forward to living with God for ever in the new heaven and new earth which He will create.

In the context of eternity, our time on earth is short. Old and New Testament writers alike compare it to a vapour:

"You have made my days a mere handbreadth; the span of my years is as nothing before you. Each man's life is but a breath." (Psalm 39:5)

"Why, you do not even know what will happen tomorrow. What is your life? You are a mist that appears for a little while and then vanishes." (James 4:14)

Although our lives here are short, the Bible makes it clear that our manner of life is important. Death may seem to be many years away, but Jesus commands us to maintain a right relationship with God, that we might lay up treasure in heaven. The way we view death, judgement and the after-life will affect the way we live our lives, and as Christians, we need to know that life is a time of training for our royal calling as eternal members of the family of God, and that we have already begun to live for eternity.

In our leisure-orientated society, it is tempting for Christians to seek a life of wealth and comfort rather than the discipline and effort of the spiritual walk, but in doing so, they remain spiritual babes who have to be fed with milk rather than with meat. They lack the spiritual robustness to overcome the trials of life. When all is well they blossom, but when difficulties come they panic and collapse. Their roots are shallow because they have avoided the training in godliness that God wants for us all.

In his second letter to Timothy, Paul, who was himself no stranger to hardship, encourages him to endure difficulty with the discipline of a soldier:

> *"Endure hardship with us like a good soldier of Christ Jesus. No-one serving as a soldier gets involved in civilian affairs – he wants to please his commanding officer."* (2 Timothy 2:3)

If we are being put through such a training programme, imagine the glory that will be ours in the age to come. As the apostle Paul writes,

> *"I consider that our present sufferings are not worth comparing with the glory that will be revealed in us."*
> (Romans 8:18)

Peter describes this hope of glory as a *"living hope"* and gives us ample grounds for rejoicing in it,

> *"Praise be to the God and Father of our Lord Jesus Christ! In his great mercy he has given us new birth into a living hope through the resurrection of Jesus Christ from the dead, and into an inheritance that can never perish, spoil or fade – kept in heaven for you, who through faith are shielded by God's power until the coming of the salvation that is ready to be revealed in the last time. In this you greatly rejoice, though now for a little while you may have had to suffer grief in all kinds of trials. These have come so that your faith – of greater worth than gold, which perishes even though refined by fire – may be proved genuine and may result in praise, glory and honour when Jesus Christ is revealed."*
> (1 Peter 1:3-7)

Therefore, whenever we have problems, whenever there are difficult circumstances, whenever we are misunderstood, whenever people gossip about us, or the workload is too heavy, we can rejoice with inexpressible joy (1 Peter 1:8).

As we grow in the knowledge of God, and experience more deeply His love, grace and faithfulness, it becomes possible to trust Him completely for the future. Then, like Paul, we will know such an assurance of our eternal destiny that we will long to enter into it.

> *"Now we know that if the earthly tent we live in is destroyed, we have a building from God, an eternal house in heaven, not built by human hands. Meanwhile we groan, longing to be clothed with our heavenly dwelling, because when we are clothed, we will not be found naked. For while we are in this tent, we groan and are burdened, because we do not wish to be unclothed but to be clothed with our heavenly dwelling, so that what is mortal may be swallowed up by life. Now it is God who has made us for this very purpose and has given us the Spirit as a deposit, guaranteeing what is to come."*
>
> (2 Corinthians 5:1-5)

Clearly, while we live in our *"earthly tents"* there will always be an element of mystery about the eternal,

> *"However, as it is written: 'No eye has seen, no ear has heard, no mind has conceived what God has prepared for those who love him' – but God has revealed it to us by his Spirit. The Spirit searches all things, even the deep things of God."*
>
> (1 Corinthians 2:9-10)

By revelation, King David could pen the following words with complete assurance that God had provided him with a glorious destiny.

> *"You will show me the path of life; In your presence is fullness of joy; At your right hand are pleasures for evermore."*
>
> (Psalm 16:11 NKJV)

Of one thing we may be sure. Now, in Christ, we have become

the objects of God's delight. He loves us all with a mighty love which has no beginning and can have no end.

> *"How great is the love the Father has lavished on us, that we should be called children of God! And that is what we are! The reason the world does not know us is that it did not know him. Dear friends, now we are children of God, and what we will be has not yet been made known. But we know that when he appears, we shall be like him, for we shall see him as he is. Everyone who has this hope in him purifies himself, just as he is pure."* (1 John 3:1-3)

Finally, let us consider two passages concerning the things which *"God has prepared for those who love Him"*. The first forms part of Jesus' words of comfort to his disciples before his death. The second is part of the revelation given to John of the events which will bring history to its consummation.

Both express what is for us a glorious desire in the heart of God to be with His people for the whole of eternity.

> *"Do not let your hearts be troubled. Trust in God; trust also in me. In my Father's house are many rooms; if it were not so, I would have told you. I am going there to prepare a place for you. And if I go and prepare a place for you, I will come back and take you to be with me that you also may be where I am."* (John 14:1-3)

> *"Then I saw a new heaven and a new earth, for the first heaven and the first earth had passed away, and there was no longer any sea. I saw the Holy City, the new Jerusalem, coming down out of heaven from God, prepared as a bride beautifully dressed for her husband. And I heard a loud voice from the throne saying, 'Now the dwelling of God is with men, and he will live with them. They will be his people, and God himself will be with them and be their God. He will wipe every tear from their eyes. There will be no more death or mourning or crying or pain, for the old order of things has passed away.'"* (Revelation 21:1-4)